This print edition collects Volumes 1 and 2 of the Jokes Against Humanity books. The material is inte possess a very flexible and accommod

Regardless, certain people may unfor jokes somewhat offensive. More ratio simply find a treasure trove of witty a

GW01465707

All characters appearing in this work are fictitious. Any resemblance to real persons, living or dead, is purely coincidental.

Printed in the United States of America

First Printing, 2016

Publication Date: February 13, 2016
Sold by: Amazon Digital Services LLC
Language: English
ISBN-13: 978-1530459902
ISBN-10: 1530459907

Ballsych Publishing
Tampa FL 33626

MHBallsych@gmail.com

To my lovely wife and kids - Hugo and Zuesie

Jokes Against Humanity

M. Harry Ballsych

Contents (Volume 2)

Jokes Against Humanity

M. Harry Ballsych

Two Nuns Go On a Bike Ride

Two nuns are out riding their bikes. On their way back to the convent, the nun in front decides to lead the other nun through the old part of town.

After a while, the nun in back calls out "Sister Beatrice, I've never come this way before."

The nun in front yells back, "I know right? It's the cobblestones!"

Mickey Mouse in Divorce Court

Mickey Mouse is in court, petitioning for a divorce from Minnie.

"Mr. Mouse," says the judge, "I'm afraid you can't petition this court for a divorce from your wife simply because you find her to be a little strange."

Mickey replies, "I didn't say she was a little strange your honor. I said she was fucking Goofy."

The Masochist

A sadist, a masochist, a murderer, a necrophile, a zoophile and a pyromaniac are all standing around the jail courtyard, when they see a cat run by.

The zoophile turns and asks the others "Hey! Let's catch that cat and have sex with it!"

"OK, you can have sex with it, but then let me torture it," says the sadist.

"OK, you can have sex with it and you can torture it, but then let me kill it," says the murderer.

"OK you can have sex with it, you torture it, and you kill it, but then let me have sex with it after," says the necrophile.

"OK you can have sex with it, you torture it, you kill it, and you have sex with it again, but then let me set it on fire," says the pyromaniac.

There was a long pause, and then the masochist says,

"…Meow!"

The Fitness Band

I received a fitness band for Christmas.

I haven't gone out jogging with it yet, but it does show I jerked off for 6 miles today.

Boy has Sex with Teacher

The mother asks her son, "What did you do at school today Harry?"

Harry answers, "I had sex with my teacher."

Upon hearing this the mother becomes very upset. When they arrive home, she tells him to go directly to his room and wait for his father to come home.

The father returns from work a couple hours later and the mother tells him what their son had said to her.

The dad walks up to his son's room and says, "Harry, mom told me what happened today. Listen don't feel bad. I'm actually sort of proud of you. What do you say we go and buy that new bicycle you wanted?"

They go and get the bike and when they bring it home the father asks, "Would you like to try it out?"

Harry replies, "Not now dad. My butt still hurts."

The Enlarged Prostate

A drunk man smelling of cheap liquor flops down on a subway seat next to a priest.

The man's shirt was stained, his face was plastered with lipstick, and he had a half-empty bottle of vodka sticking out of his torn coat pocket. He opens a newspaper and began reading.

After a few minutes the man turns to the priest and asks, "Say Father, what causes an enlarged prostate?"

The priest replies, "My Son, it's caused by lack of faith, being with wicked women, too much alcohol, contempt for your fellow man, sleeping around with prostitutes and lack of proper hygiene."

The drunk muttered in response, "Well, I'll be dammed," returning to his paper.

The priest, thinking about what he had said, nudged the man and apologized: "I'm very sorry. I didn't mean to come on so strong. How long have you had an enlarged prostate?"

The drunk answered, "I don't have that! I was just reading here that the Pope does!"

The Deaf Couple

A deaf couple is working on an arrangement on how best to communicate when they want to have sex.

The wife writes, "Harry, if you want to have sex, squeeze my left tit once. If you don't want to have sex, squeeze my right tit twice."

The husband writes "OK Henrietta, and if you want to have sex, pull my dick once. If you don't want to have sex, pull my dick 137 times."

Old Man at the Jewelry Store

An old man walks into a jewelry store with a very hot young blonde in his arms. He tells the owner he is looking for a very special ring for his new girlfriend.

The jeweler looks through his stock and brings out a $5,000 ring.

The old man says, "No, no, I'd like to see something a little more special please."

The owner goes out back and brings out another ring. "Here's a stunning ring for $40,000," he says.

The lady's eyes sparkle and her whole body shakes with excitement.

The old man notices this and says, "We'll take it!"

The jeweler asks how payment will be made and the old man says, "By check. I'll make it out now and you can call the bank Monday to verify the funds; I'll pick the ring up Monday afternoon."

On Monday morning, the jeweler angrily phones the old man and says, "Sir...That check you gave me, it's no good!"

"I know!" says the old man, "…but let me tell you about my weekend!"

The Pacifier

Two gay men decide to have a baby. They mix their sperm and have a surrogate mother artificially inseminated.

When the baby is born, they rush to the hospital. They find fourteen newborn babies in the ward and all but one are crying hysterically.

A nurse comes by, and to the men's delight, points out that the one happy quiet child in the corner is theirs.

"Isn't it wonderful?" Lance exclaims to Brad his partner. "All these unhappy children, and ours is so happy."

'Oh he's happy now," says the nurse. "But just wait until we take the pacifier out of his ass."

Harry's Cat

Harry returns home late one night after spending time with his mistress.

As he is getting ready for bed he notices in the mirror that his lover had made large scratches down his back with her nails when they were having sex.

Worried that his wife will notice, he gets an idea and as the cat enters the bathroom he runs to it and kicks it hard against the wall.

"MMMEEEEEOOOOOWWWWW!!!!" the cat wails in pain and scurries away.

The wife, who was already in bed, hears the commotion and comes running.

"What just happened!?" She exclaims.

"Nothing, nothing, just that stupid cat. I had to punish him because he jumped on me and gave me this big scratch down my back."

"Oh yes! Yes! Punish him good! Earlier tonight he left me with this huge hickey on my neck!

Wife Like That

Harry and his buddy Hank are having a few beers at the bar.

Suddenly out the blue, Hank says to Harry, "I'm getting a divorce from my wife. It's been nearly three months now that she's hardly uttered a single word to me.

Harry takes a swig from his beer and calmly replies:

"Think it through Hank. Wife like that are almost impossible to find."

Fart Football

Harry and his wife are in bed when he suddenly farts and says,

"7 points!"

His wife rolls over and says, "What in the world did you just say?"

Harry replies "Its fart football."

A few minutes later his wife lets one go and says, "Touchdown, tie score!"

Five minutes later Harry lets another one go and says, "Aha! I'm now ahead 14 to 7!"

Not to be outdone, the wife rips out another one and says, "Touchdown again! - tie score!"

Five seconds go by and she lets out a little squeaker and says, 'Field goal! Now I lead 17 to 14!"

Now the pressure is on for Harry. He refuses to get beaten by his little lady, so he strains very hard. He gives it everything he's got, and in doing so he accidentally lets out a shart and shits the bed!

The wife, noticing a strange smell asks, "What the hell was that?"

Harry smiles and says, "Half time, switch sides!"

A Rich Old Guy Goes Golfing

A rich old guy goes golfing and brings along a gorgeous young lady in a tight mini skirt.

"Hi guys, meet my new fiancée," he says, beaming with pride.

For the rest of the afternoon his friends can't take their eyes off the young beauty.

After the round of golf, the rich man goes up to the bar to order drinks for the group. One of his friends accompanies him and quietly asks: "Dude, how did you manage to hook up with such a hot young lady? I mean you're pushing seventy and she must be at least forty years younger than you!"

"I lied about my age"

"She believed you!? How old did you say you were?"

"I told her I was ninety six."

Lost Wife at the Supermarket

An old man loses his wife at the supermarket.

He approaches a very beautiful woman and says to her, "Excuse me, I've lost my wife somewhere in this supermarket. Can you please stand here and pretend to talk with me for a couple of minutes?"

The woman looked puzzled. "I don't understand," she says, "why do you want me to talk to you?"

"Well you see it's because every time I stop to talk to a woman with tits and ass like yours, my wife has a tendency to show up out of nowhere!"

A Drunk Walks into a Bar

A drunk walks into a bar, and after staring for some time at the only woman seated at the bar, walks over to her and kisses her.

She jumps up and slaps him. He immediately apologizes and explains, "I'm sorry. I thought you were my wife. I mean you look exactly like her!"

"I bet I do you worthless, drunk piece of shit!" she yells back.

"Wow!" he mutters, "you even *sound* exactly like her!"

Late to the Funeral

Recently, I was asked by a funeral director to play at a graveside service for a homeless man at 11:00 am at a new cemetery in the suburbs. I was not familiar with the area, and my GPS did not recognize the address and so I quickly became lost.

I finally arrived, over an hour late, and saw that the family had evidently left and the funeral director and hearse were nowhere in sight. Only the digging crew was left and they were eating their lunch.

I felt badly and apologized to the men for being so late.

I went to the side of the grave and looked down and saw the vault lid was already in place.

I didn't know what else to do. I felt terrible having missed this poor man's service. So I took out my pipes and started to play.

Soon, the workers put down their lunches and began to gather around.

I played my heart and soul out for this nameless man. I played like I've never played before.

Finally, as I played 'Amazing Grace,' the workers began to weep.

They wept, I wept, and we all wept together. It was somber, and yet, we were together as one.

When I finished, I packed up my bagpipes and started for my car. Though my head hung low, my heart was full.

As I opened the door to my car, I heard one of the workers say, "I never seen nothing like that before and I've been putting in septic tanks for twenty years!"

A Young Artist

A young artist is exhibiting his first painting and it just happens that a well-known art critic is in attendance.

The critic says to the young artist, "would you like my opinion on your work?"

"Yes, of course!" says the young artist.

"Well it's absolutely worthless!" says the critic.

The young artist replies, "I know, but please tell me anyways."

Little Timmy

A 3rd grade class goes to the swimming pool on a field trip.
The lifeguard asks the class, "Do any of you know how to swim?"

Little Timmy answers: "I do! I do!"

The thing is, little Timmy has no arms and just one leg, so the lifeguard doesn't really believe him, but little Timmy insists, "I do, I do!"

The lifeguard finally lets him try.

Unexpectedly, little Timmy jumps in and swims very well to the other side of the pool and back.

The lifeguard, somewhat surprised, asks, "Wow! Where did you learn to swim like that?!"

Little Timmy says, "When I was little, each weekend my father would bring me to the coast, throw me in the deep water and I would swim back to the shore."

The lifeguard says, "Sounds a little bit harsh for a swimming lesson, don't you think?"

Little Timmy replies, "Oh no, it's not that big a deal. The most difficult part was getting out of the plastic bag each time."

Teacher in Sex Education

A teacher in sex education class starts out by drawing a penis on the chalk board and asks the class, "Does anyone know what this is?"

Little Harry says, "Yes, my dad has 2 of them!"

The teacher says, "Are you sure about that?"

And little Harry says, "Yes mam, I've seen them! He uses a small skinny one to pee with, and a big long one to brush our babysitter's teeth."

Mother Shark

A mother shark is teaching her young how to eat humans.

"First, you go straight at them and then you circle them.

Then you go straight at them again and circle them again.

Finally, you go straight at them and then you eat them."

"But, mom, why can't I just eat them the first time around?" asks one of the young sharks.

"Well, I suppose you could," she replies, "but why would you want to eat them with all the shit and piss still inside?"

Bet with the Wife

I bet my wife that she could not think of something to tell me that would make me both happy and sad at the same time.

She thought for a second and then told me I had the biggest dick of all my friends.

Jack and Mike

Jack says to his friend Mike, "Mike I'm sleeping with the Minister's wife. You think you can keep him busy for an hour or so after service Sunday?"

Mike doesn't like it, but being a good friend, he agrees to do so.

Following the service, Mike asks the minister all sorts of silly questions about the sermon, just to keep him occupied.

After a while of this, the minister gets suspicious and asks Mike what he's really up to.

Mike, feeling guilty, confesses, "Minister, my friend is sleeping with your wife right now, and he asked me to keep you occupied. I'm terribly sorry."

The minister thinks for a minute, smiles, puts a fatherly hand on Mike's shoulder and says, "You probably should hurry on home now. My wife died three years ago."

Three Women go to Heaven

Three women die and go to Heaven. They are greeted by St. Peter at the pearly gates. He welcomes them and says "Be very careful, there are many ducks in heaven. If you happen to step on any you will be punished."

The women proceed to walk in and immediately the first one steps on a duck. Right away one of the ugliest men in existence gets chained to her for eternity as punishment.

After about a week, the second woman also steps on a duck. Another extremely ugly man is chained to her for eternity as punishment.

The third woman, however, never steps on a duck and yet the most beautiful man she had ever seen gets chained to her.

"What did I do to deserve such a nice looking man?" she asks St. Peter.

St. Peter looks at her and says, "He stepped on a duck."

A Priest is walking by a Country Road

A priest is walking by a country road when he is stopped by a policeman in his cruiser. The priest asks, "What seems to be the problem, officer?"

The policeman replies, "A Boy Scout was abducted in the area, and we are looking for a potential child molester."

The priest thinks for a second, and says, "I'll do it."

The Silent Fart

Harry and his wife are kneeling in church when the old lady leans over and whispers, "Harry I just let out a really big silent fart. I'm afraid it's going to start smelling terribly. What should I do?"

Harry replies, "I suggest you get the batteries in your hearing aid replaced."

A Couple Watching TV

An elderly couple was at home watching TV. Hank had the remote and was flipping back and forth between a fishing channel and the porn channel.

Wilma was on the couch knitting. Each time she would look up at the TV...click! -the fishing channel. She would look back down to her knitting...click! -the porn channel. Look up...click! -the fishing channel. This went on for several minutes.

Wilma became more and more annoyed with each flip of the channel and finally says, "For Pete's sake, Hank... leave it on the porn channel... you already know how to fish!"

Wife sends me a Romantic Text

My wife sent me this romantic text this evening:

"If you are sleeping, send me your dreams."

"If you are laughing, send me your smile."

"If you are eating, send me a bite."

"If you are drinking send me a sip."

"If you are crying, send me your tears."

"I love you!"

To which I replied:

"I'm on the toilet. Please advise."

Use the Backdoor

I met a girl at the local bar and she took me back to her place where things proceeded to get hot and heavy very quickly.

I bent her over the kitchen table and started going at it when suddenly we heard the front door open.

"Oh shit! It's my boyfriend!" she exclaimed, "Quick, use the backdoor!"

I probably should have left right then and there...but you just don't get an offer like that every day.

The Semen Sample

The doctor gives an old man a jar and says, "Take this jar home and bring back a semen sample tomorrow."

The next day the old man returns to the doctor's office and gives him the jar, which is as empty as when he had left the office the previous day.

The doctor asks what happened and the man explains, "Well, doc, it's like this--first I tried with my right hand, but nothing. Then I tried with my left hand, and still nothing. Then I asked my wife for help.

She tried with her right hand, then with her left, still nothing. She tried with her mouth, first with her teeth in, then with her teeth out, still nothing. We even called up Wilma, the next door lady, and she tried too, first with both hands, then an armpit. She even tried squeezing it between her knees, but still nothing."

The doctor was shocked! "You asked your neighbor?"

The old man replied, "Yep! None of us could get the jar open."

The Documentary

A couple was watching a TV documentary about an African tribe. They learned that when each male member of this particular tribe reaches a certain age, he gets a string with a weight attached around his penis. After some weeks, the weight stretches the penis until its 20 inches long.

Later that evening, as the man was getting out of the shower, his wife says, "Harry, why don't we try the African string and weight technique?"

Harry agrees, and they tie a string with a weight to his penis.

A few days later his wife asks, "How is our little experiment coming along?"

Harry replies "Well, it looks like we're about halfway there."

The wife, excited, asks, "You mean it's already grown to 10 inches?"

"No," Harry replies, "It's turning black."

The Magic Mirror

A man finds a magic mirror and gets excited to have his wish come true.

He chants: Magic Mirror on the Wall, make my penis touch the floor!

Poof!

His penis touches the floor.

His legs are also shorter. Way shorter.

The Sponge Bath

Two nurses are giving a woman in a coma a sponge bath. They notice that whenever they get near her private areas that she starts to get a little aroused.

They theorize that perhaps a little oral sex will help to bring her out of the coma. They go out to the lobby and share their theory with her husband.

The husband is a little apprehensive at first, but he agrees to do it.

The nurses leave the man with his wife and give him some privacy.

They return 10 minutes later and find that the woman is dead!

"What happened?" asks one of the nurses. The husband replies, "I don't know...I think she choked!"

Wine at Le Meurice

An older man walks into the famous restaurant Le Meurice in Paris. He orders a bottle of Rothschild Mouton 1928.

The waiter returns with a full bottle of wine and pours a small amount in a tasting glass. The man barely smells the wine before putting the glass down and says, "This is NOT a 1928 Mouton!"

Soon, almost 10 people are standing around the table. This includes the chef and the restaurants' owner. Every single one is trying to convince the old man that it is, in fact, a 1928 Mouton.

The waiter asks: "Sir, how can you be so sure this isn't a 1928 Mouton?"

The older man responds, "Because my name is Phillip de Rothschild, and I and my family produce Mouton wine!"

Upon hearing this, the owner admits that the wine is actually a Clerc Milon 1928. He explains, "I assure you sir that we intended no deception. The Clerc Milon is produced in the exact same village, with the exact same grapes, uses the same type of baskets and both are aged in the exact same types of barrels. The wines are exactly the same! The only difference is that the vineyards are on the opposite side of the village."

Mr. Rothschild turns to the owner and says, "When you get home tonight, ask your wife to undress. I want you to then put one finger inside her cunt and one finger inside her ass. Pull them out, and smell them. You'll then understand the importance of a small geographical difference!"

Drug Dealer and Prostitute

Q- What's the difference between a drug dealer and a prostitute?

A- A prostitute can wash her crack and sell it again

Monkey in Tree

A man notices a monkey has climbed up his backyard tree.

He goes online and finds a man who specializes in monkey trapping and removal.

When the trapper arrives at the house he shows up with a stick, a set of handcuffs, a Chihuahua, and a shotgun.

He tells the homeowner "I'm going to climb up in the tree and use this stick to hit the monkey until it falls out of the tree. When it lands, the trained Chihuahua will viciously lunge for the monkey's genitals and when it attempts to protect himself I will slap on the handcuffs."

The homeowner, a little confused, says "That's crazy enough it just might work, but what's the shotgun for?"

"In case I fall out of the tree first....you must then shoot the Chihuahua."

The European Commission

The European Commission has just announced an agreement whereby English will be the official language of the European Union rather than German which had been the second option.

As part of the negotiations, the British Government conceded that English spelling had some room for improvement and has accepted a 5- year phase-in plan that would become known as "Euro-English".

In the first year, "s" will replace the soft "c". Sertainly, this will make the sivil servants jump with joy. The hard "c" will be dropped in favour of "k". This should klear up konfusion, and keyboards kan have one less letter.

There will be growing publik enthusiasm in the sekond year when the troublesome "ph" will be replaced with "f". This will make words like fotograf 20% shorter.

In the 3rd year, publik akseptanse of the new spelling kan be expekted to reach the stage where more komplikated changes are possible.

Governments will enkourage the removal of double letters which have always ben a deterent to akurate speling.

Also, al wil agre that the horibl mes of the silent "e" in the languag is disgrasful and it should go away.
By the 4th yer people wil be reseptiv to steps such as replasing "th" with "z" and "w" with "v".

During ze fifz yer, ze unesesary "o" kan be dropd from vords kontaining "ou" and after ziz fifz yer, ve vil hav a reil sensibl riten styl.

Zer vil be no mor trubl or difikultis and evrivun vil find it ezi tu understand ech oza. Ze drem of a united urop vil finali kum tru.

Concerned about Wife

I'm beginning to get more than a little concerned about my wife.

Lately, she begins every conversation with "Harry, were you even listening to me?"

Golfer and Skydiver

Q- What's the difference between a bad golfer and a bad skydiver?

A- The bad golfer goes "whack!" followed by "Dammit!"

The bad skydiver goes "Dammit!" Followed by "whack!"

Jewish Samurai

There once was a powerful Japanese emperor who needed a new chief samurai. So he sent out a declaration throughout the entire nation that he was searching for a chief.

A year passes, and only three people apply for the very demanding position: a Japanese samurai, a Chinese samurai, and a Jewish samurai.

The emperor asks the Japanese samurai to come in and demonstrate why he should be the chief samurai. The Japanese samurai opens a matchbox, and out flies a bumblebee. Whoosh! Went his sword.

The bumblebee drops dead, sliced in half.

The emperor exclaims, "That is very impressive!"

The emperor then issues the same challenge to the Chinese samurai.

The Chinese samurai also opens a matchbox and out flies a fly. Whoosh, whoosh, whoosh, whoosh! The fly drops dead, sliced into four equal pieces.

The emperor exclaims, "That is very impressive!"

Now the emperor turns to the Jewish samurai, and asks him to demonstrate why he should be the chief samurai.

The Jewish Samurai opens a matchbox as well, and out flies a gnat. His flashing sword goes Whoosh! but the gnat is still alive and flying around.

The emperor, obviously disappointed, says, "Very ambitious, but why is that gnat not yet dead?"

The Jewish Samurai smiles and says, "Circumcision is not meant to kill."

Happy Birthday

Today was my birthday. At breakfast I was hoping my wife would be pleasant and say, "Happy Birthday!", and possibly have a small present for me. She barely said good morning, let alone "Happy Birthday."

I thought... Well, that's marriage for you, but the kids... they will remember.
My kids also didn't say a word. When I left for the office, I was feeling pretty sad.

As I walked into my office, my secretary Lisa said, "Good Morning boss, and Happy Birthday!" It felt a little better that at least someone had remembered.

I worked until one o'clock, when Jane knocked on my door and said, "You know, it's such a beautiful day outside, and it's your Birthday, what you say we go out to lunch, just you and me."

I said, "Thanks, Lisa, that's the greatest thing I've heard all day. Let's go!"

On the way to lunch she said, "Let's drop by my apartment, it's just around the corner." I said "Sure."

After arriving at her apartment, Jane turned to me and said, "Boss, if you don't mind, I'm going to step into the bedroom for just a minute. I'll be right back."

"Okay," I nervously replied.

She went into the bedroom and, after a couple of minutes, she came out carrying a huge birthday cake, followed by my wife, my kids, and dozens of my friends and co-workers, all singing "Happy birthday".

And I just sat there...

On the couch...

sobbing...

naked...
and erect.

Krishna

Krishna was trying to get a tech support job in India. The Personnel Manager said, "Krishna, you need to show you are proficient in the English language. Please make a sentence using the words: yellow, pink, and green."

Krishna responded, "The telephone goes green, green, I pink it up, and say, Yellow! This is Krishna!"

The Baby Grand Piano

Four men are having to carry a baby grand piano to the 10th floor of an old apartment building that has no lift.

As they make their way up the stairs they start to get very tired and lose track of how many floors they've climbed.

They decide to have one of the men climb up to the apartment and then come back down and let them know how many more floors they still need to climb.

The man goes up the remaining stairs and when he gets to the 10th floor, he looks around and calculates that he went up 6 flights so he must have started from the 4th floor.

He makes his way back to the other men and says, "Boys I have two pieces of bad news."

One of the men replies, "Shit! How 'bout you tell us just one of the bad news and when we get this fucking piano to the 10th floor you can tell us the other."

"OK, we still have 6 more floors to go."

The men groan and continue to climb up the stairs until finally they arrive at the tenth floor.

"We made it! What was that other piece of bad news?"

"This ain't the right building!"

The Negligee

A husband walks into Victoria's Secret to purchase a sheer negligee for his wife. He is shown several styles that range from $250 to $500 in price -- the sheerer, the higher the price.

Naturally, he opts for the sheerest item, pays the $500, and takes it home. He presents it to his wife and asks her to go upstairs, put it on, and model it for him.

Upstairs the wife sees the price tag and how sheer the negligee is. She thinks – This is so sheer that it might as well be nothing. I'll model it naked, return it tomorrow, and keep the $500 for myself.'

She appears naked on the balcony and strikes a seductive pose.

The husband says, "Good Grief! You'd think for $500, they'd at least iron it!"

8 Year old Zuesie

Little 8 year old Zuesie is in her back yard digging a hole. Her neighbor Mrs. Johnson hears her crying and peeks over the fence and says "Gee Zuesie, what's going on?"

Zuesie says "I'm digging a hole, Mrs. Johnson"

Mrs. Johnson asks "I can see that, and why are you digging a hole?"

Zuesie replies "I'm burying my dead gold fish."

Mrs. Johnson laughs and asks "Oh I see...and why are you making the hole so big?"

Zuesie replies "Because my goldfish is inside your fucking cat."

Pinocchio's Splinters

Every time Pinocchio and his girlfriend had sex, she would complain about splinters inside her the following day.

Eventually, Pinocchio goes to see Geppetto for help.

Geppetto tells Pinocchio to go to the hardware store and buy some fine sandpaper to sand off the splinters before he has sex with his girlfriend.

A week later, Geppetto sees Pinocchio, busily sanding away at his splinters, "So how's it going with your girlfriend?" Asks Geppetto.

Pinocchio replies. "Girlfriend? Who needs a girlfriend?"

The End

Enjoy the jokes? Follow me on Twitter at

www.twitter.com/M_H_Ballsych

Let me know your favorites and why!

Also Volume 2 and Volume 3 of Jokes Against Humanity are now available in the Amazon store!

http://www.amazon.com/gp/product/B01C7VEJFQ

http://www.amazon.com/gp/product/B01DFTLZIS

Jokes Against Humanity

Vol 2

M. Harry Ballsych

A Woman Goes to the Pharmacy

A woman visits the local drug store and tells the pharmacist, "Sir, I'd like a poison that will kill my husband, but it needs to look as if he died of natural causes."

The pharmacist frowns at this and says, "Ma'am, not only will I not do that for you, but I'm afraid I must now report this request of yours to the authorities!"

The woman reaches into her purse, pulls out a photograph and hands it to the pharmacist. It's a picture of her husband having sex with the pharmacist's wife.

The pharmacist hands it back to her and says "Ma'am, you should have clarified that you brought a prescription!"

The Golden Bellybutton

A boy from a very religious family had been born with a golden bellybutton with a perfectly vertical crease running down the middle.

His parents were convinced this was a sign from God and were always proud of their son and his peculiar golden bellybutton.

The poor boy, however, grew tired of all the kids constantly making fun of his golden bellybutton.

Given his religious upbringing, one day he finally grew the courage to pray to God requesting that his bellybutton be made normal.

He prayed for this continuously for many hours until suddenly the clouds parted, and what appeared to be a golden screwdriver could be seen descending from the heavens.

The boy watched in awe and wonder as the golden tool drew closer, until at last it mated with the crease in his bellybutton and began to turn.

After three turns the bellybutton became loose, and both it, and the tool, retreated back to the heavens.

The boy was overcome with joy! His golden bellybutton was now gone, and as he stood up to go tell his family about this great miracle, his ass fell off.

From the Waist Down

A woman learns that her husband has been involved in a terrible accident. She arrives at the hospital and meets with the attending doctor. She asks, "Doctor! I came here as quickly as possible. How is my husband?"

The doctor replies, "Well Miss, from the waist down he appears fine."

The woman, somewhat relieved, asks again, "…and from the waist up?"

The Doctor answers. "I'm afraid I wouldn't know because they haven't brought in that part yet."

Vandilo and Silvanus

Two gypsies, Vandilo and Silvanus, are arguing with each other as to who is more skilled at stealing.

They decide to test their craft at the local bakery. They agree that whoever walks out with the most stolen goods gets bragging rights.

The first gypsy, Vandilo, walks in and casually asks the owner if bus # 20 stops at the corner.

The owner, leery of the gypsy, looks him over carefully and then searches on his phone for the bus routes. As he does this, Vandilo deftly grabs a pastry and sticks it in his pocket. The owner confirms that bus # 20 stops at the corner without noticing the theft.

Vandilo then asks him for the time. As the owner looks down at his watch, Vandilo again swiftly grabs a second pastry and also drops it into his pocket.

He then asks the owner for some change for the bus. Again, as the owner is distracted making change, Vandilo grabs a third pastry.

At this point Silvanus walks in the store. He says to the owner "Sir, if you give me a pastry, my friend and I will show you a fantastic magic trick."

Intrigued by this, the owner accepts the offer and gives him a pastry. Silvanus swallows it and asks for another one. The owner gives him another one. Silvanus swallows that one as well and asks for a third pastry and proceeds to eats that, too.

The owner now starts to grow suspicious about this so called magic trick and threatens the gypsies, "If you don't tell me what this magic trick is about, or pay me for my pastries, I'm going to call the police!"

Silvanus replies, "Wait! Wait…now look in my friend's pockets!"

The Taxi Driver

A man hails a taxi cab and asks the cabbie to take him to a nearby motel. Once they arrive there he thanks the cabbie and asks "Would you like to earn an additional $500 dollars?"

The cabbie replies, 'Of course I would! What do you need me to do?"

"You see that couple there entering the motel?" The man asks.

"I do…" answers the cabbie.

"Well that happens to be my wife with her boyfriend. Go in there, get her out and bring her to me!" requests the man.

"For 500 dollars?" The cabbie asks.

"For 500 dollars. You have my word," says the man.

Right then, the cabbie gets out of the taxi, enters the motel and a minute later comes out dragging a screaming naked woman by the hair back to the taxi.

The man, panicking, yells at the cabbie, "Hey! What the fuck are you doing?! That's not my wife! You saw my wife! She's a brunette and she went in wearing a black dress!"

The cabbie responds, "Yes I know! This is *my* wife! I'll go back in for yours in a minute!"

Man Goes to Confession

A man goes to confession. "Forgive me father for I have sinned. Last week I stole my neighbor's chicken and ate it for dinner."

The priest says to the man, "God forgives you my son. For penance, say two Hail Mary's and give $20 - the value of the chicken - to the first person you come across. Tell them God loves them. Now you may go in peace."

The man says his prayers, exits the confessional, and on his way out of the church sees a pretty young lady walking in. He approaches her, reaches into his wallet and hands her $20.

Before he could say 'God loves you', she looks up at the man and says, "I'm sorry, but I don't do anything for $20. Its $50 or nothing!"

The man, confused, explains to the lady, "The Father just told me I should give you $20."

The lady says, "The Father yes, but you must understand he's been a steady client for many years!"

The Parrot from the Brothel

A lady goes to the pet store to buy a parrot. She sees a very nice looking parrot on sale and walks up to the sales attendant. 'Excuse me,' she says, "I would like to see about buying this parrot."

The attendant explains that the parrot had belonged to the Madam at the local brothel that was shut down by the police the prior week. He explains the parrot is very smart and knows how to say quite a few words, but he is prone to profanity. Hence the deep discount.

The lady thinks about it and figures that in her religious household the parrot would quickly forget his bad language and acquire a cleaner vocabulary.

She says to the sales clerk, "I'll take my chances with this one. He's a beautiful parrot. My husband, Rick will be thrilled!"

She takes the parrot home and lifts the drape off the cage.

The parrot looks around the room and at the lady and says,

"New house, new Madam! BRAAAAK!"

The lady laughs and calls out for her daughters to greet their new pet. The girls come down and when the parrot sees them, says,

"New house, new Madam, new whores! BRAAAAK!"

The daughters break out in laughter, and the mother blushes with embarrassment.

Finally, the father returns home from work and is shown the parrot by the family

The parrot sees the father and says,

"New house, new Madam, new whores, same John. Hello Rick! BRAAAAK!!!"

The Japanese Assistant

A man goes to visit his friend in Japan. They meet at the friend's Tokyo office.

"Bro! How you been doing?" he asks his friend.

"I'm doing great my friend, and you?" replies his friend.

"I bet you are! Especially judging by that hot ass secretary of yours!" he tells the friend.

"Oh that? Well, you won't believe it, but she's actually a robot. "

"A robot! How in the world is that fine piece of ass a robot?"

"Look! I'll show you." They walk over to the secretary. The friend squeezes her left breast and she starts to take dictation. Then he squeezes her right breast and she begins to put stamps on envelopes.

"Wow! That is absolutely amazing!" says the visitor.

"That's not all. I programmed her to have sex and she is absolutely amazing!" the friend says.

"Shut the front door! For real?"

"For real! In fact, why don't I leave you two alone for a little while and you can see for yourself?"

The man lets his visiting friend have some fun with his secretary, but after several minutes he hears an ear piercing scream coming from his buddy. He opens the door and sees his friend holding his bleeding groin and rolling on the floor in pain.

"Aw shit! … I'm so sorry! I forgot to tell you that her rear end is a pencil sharpener!"

Together at Last

Maria, being a devout Catholic, was married at an early age and had 10 children.

After her first husband died, she remarried and went on to have 10 more children.

A few weeks after her second husband died, Maria also passed away.

At Maria's funeral, the priest looked skyward and said, "At last, they're finally together."

After the eulogy, her sister went up to the priest "Excuse me, Father, but did you mean she and her first husband are now together, or she and her second husband?"

The priest replied, "I meant her legs."

The Escaped Convict

A hardened criminal serving a life sentence for rape and 1st degree murder escapes from prison after spending 25 years behind bars.

On the run, he breaks into and enters a house where he finds a young couple sleeping. The inmate binds the man to a chair and ties the woman to the bed. He then puts his face close to the young lady's neck and suddenly gets up and goes into the bathroom.

Immediately, the young husband drags his chair over to the bedside and whispers to his wife,

"Sweetie, this man is a desperate and dangerous criminal who has not been with a woman in years. I saw him kissing your neck. I know it's difficult, but I beg you to please cooperate with him and do everything he asks of you. If he forces you to have sex do not resist him. Do not disobey, or make him angry in any way! Our lives depend on it! You understand don't you? I love you!"

The young wife then whispers to her husband, "Honey I'm so glad you feel this way. You're right that he's not been with a woman in years, but he was not kissing my neck. He was telling me that he likes you and wanted to know if we keep any Vaseline in the bathroom. Be strong my love. I love you too!"

The Boss's Advice

An employee shows up to work looking rather upset and with a worried look after he found his cat had been run over by a car earlier that morning and then himself getting into a fender bender as he drove to work.

Being that he is one of the best employees at the firm, the boss calls him into his office and asks him what's bothering him.

The boss hears the employee explain his tragic news of the loss of his pet and the accident that he got into afterwards.

The boss then proceeds to give the employee some advice. "Whenever I'm having a particularly difficult day like obviously you are today, I just leave work and go to my home. I take a good long shower, then I sip some single malt whiskey and make love to my wife. No matter how crappy I felt before, I feel like a new man afterwards.

The employee nods his head, thanks the boss and proceeds to take the rest of the day off as his boss suggested.

The next day the employee shows up to work with a spring in his step, and wearing an ear to ear grin.

The boss sees him and says, "Aha! I see you took my advice! Works like a charm doesn't it?"

"Absolutely! By the time I got home yesterday afternoon I felt like a new man. By the way, your wife is absolutely amazing!"

Young Indian Visits the Brothel

A young Indian knocks on the door to the local brothel.

The Madam answers the door and asks the Indian, "What can I do for you?"

The Indian replies "Indian want woman!"

The Madam asks, "Very well. Are you experienced?"

"No, first time," answers the young Indian.

"Well, I'm afraid our ladies are not cheap and if you are not experienced you may be wasting your money. I suggest you seek a tree with a small hole and practice for a month or so and then come back. OK?" says the Madam.

The Indian goes and practices for a month with a tree. When he returns to the brothel he also brings a very thick wooden stick.

The Indian knocks on the brothel door and again the Madam answers.

"Indian want woman. Have experience." Explains the Indian.

The Madam allows the Indian inside, negotiates a price, and calls Gertrude down. Gertrude and the Indian go up to her room. She undresses and climbs up on the bed.

Suddenly the Indian gives Gertrude a tremendous whack on her ass with his stick.

WHAACK!

Gertrude screamed with both surprise and pain and cusses at the Indian as she rubbed her behind, "What the FUCK was that for you stupid Indian!?"

The Indian answered, "Indian want to make sure no wasps in hole."

The Parrot from the Brothel (Part 2)

A lady walks over to the priest after Sunday service.

"Father, I wanted to apologize for not offering our home this year for the bible study sessions."

The priest says, "Oh that's quite alright my child, I don't expect this to be a recurring intrusion on anyone's home. I'm sure someone else will come forward."

"Well you see father, the thing is I acquired a pet parrot earlier this year that was raised in a house of ill repute. As you can imagine she managed to pick up a very foul vocabulary. We just haven't been able to train her to not say bad words so we have been too embarrassed to have visitors over to the house."

"You don't say!" said the priest. "I happen to have a parrot as well! but mine was raised here in the rectory and happens to be a very Catholic parrot. I've even taught it to pray with me 3 times daily!" Boasted the priest. "Perhaps I can bring my parrot over and let them be together for a few weeks and he can discipline your parrot and teach her the ways of the church!" suggested the priest.

"What a wonderful idea father! That would be so generous of you!" replied the lady.

"Very well, I can come by this evening if you'd like."

"Please do," replied the lady.

The priest arrives at the house later that evening with his parrot. The lady's parrot sees the priest's parrot and says,

"Handsome parrot! Wanna fuck? BRAAAAK!"

The priest's parrot removes his rosary necklace, closes his eyes, bows down his head and says,

"Thank you Lord for answering my prayers BRAAAAK!"

Your Way of Thinking

Little Tommy was sitting in class doing his math problems when his teacher asks him:

"Tommy, if there are five birds up in a bush and a hunter shoots one with a gun, how many birds would be left in the bush?"

"None," replied Tommy, "because one would die and the other four would fly away."

"Well, the answer I was looking for was four, but I do love your way of thinking," said the teacher.

Then Tommy said, "I have a question for you, Miss Jameson."

"Is that so? Let's hear it!" said the teacher.

"Three ladies are sitting on a bench eating ice cream. The first lady is licking it, the second lady is biting it, and the third one is sucking on it. Which of the three ladies is married?"

The teacher blushed and sheepishly replied. "Well, I'm not sure ... I suppose the one that is sucking on her ice cream?" she replied.

"No. The married lady is the one wearing the wedding ring on her finger..., but I do love your way of thinking!"

Where Do Taxi Drivers Come From?

A lady was riding in a taxi cab along with her five year old daughter.

They pass by a corner, and the little girl sees a group of prostitutes wearing very tight miniskirts. Curious, she asks her mother:

"Mommy, who are those ladies?"

Nervously, the mother answers:

"Those are ladies who are waiting for their husbands to return home from work, my dear."

The driver, who had been listening tells the mother:

"Ma'am, you should tell the child the truth. They are prostitutes!"

After a tense silence, the little girl asks another question:

"Mommy, do prostitutes have children?"

The mother replied "Of course dear! Where do you suppose taxi drivers come from?"

The Mistress

A husband and his wife are having dinner at a very fancy restaurant when an absolutely stunning young woman comes over to their table, gives the husband a big wet kiss on the lips, then says she'll see him later and walks away.

□□□□□□□□□□□□□□□□□□□□□□□□□□□

The wife glares at her husband and says, "Who the hell was that?"

"Who? That lady?" replies the husband, "She's my mistress."

"Well, that's the last straw!" says the wife. "I've had enough of this! I demand a divorce!"

"Remember honey, if you and I get divorced it will mean no more shopping trips to Paris, no more wintering in Aruba, no more summers in Fiji, no more Porsche in the garage, and no more country club membership. Not only that, but no more fancy diamonds, no more credit card, and no large bank account. But," he added, "I suppose the decision is all yours."

Just then, a mutual friend of theirs enters the restaurant with a gorgeous babe on his arm.

"Who's that woman with Andy?" asks the wife.

"That's his mistress," says the husband.

"Ours is prettier!" she replies.

Foul-Mouthed Old Man at the Bank

An old man walks into a bank and says to the lady at the teller window "I want to open a fucking checking account."

The lady replies, "I beg your pardon Sir! I must have misunderstood you. What did you just say?"

"Listen up, dammit. I'm not repeating myself again. I said I want to open a fucking checking account now!"

"I'm very sorry sir, but that kind of language is not tolerated in this bank." Said the offended teller.

The teller leaves the window and hurries over to the bank manager to inform him of her situation. The manager assures the teller that he will deal with the disrespectful customer.

They both return to the window and the manager asks the old man, "Sir, what seems to be the problem?"

"There is no fucking problem," the old man says. "I just won 20 million dollars in the fucking lottery and I need to open a fucking checking account in this fucking bank so the state can deposit my fucking winnings!"

"I see…," says the manager, "…and I gather this fucking bitch is giving you a fucking hard time?"

A Lesbian's Bed

Q- How many screws are needed to hold together a lesbian's bed?

A- None. It's all Tongue and Groove.

The Flash

The Flash was out doing his daily laps around Central Park one morning, when he sees Wonder Woman lying on the grass behind some bushes sunning herself and wearing nothing from the waist down.

He thinks to himself, 'You know, with my super speed, I bet I can go right up to her, fuck her brains out, and leave before she even realizes what happened!'

Almost instantly, he takes his suit off and starts picking up more and more speed as he runs laps around the park. Soon he is just a barely visible blur. As he reaches his maximum speed, he dashes towards Wonder Woman, mounts her, bangs away 60 thrusts, and pulls away just as fast as he came!

"Ouch!" "Dammit!" "Ouuuuch!"

"What's wrong babe?" asked Wonder Woman.

"I'm not exactly sure, but I suddenly felt as if somebody had just fucked me up the ass!" said the Invisible Man.

Wendy

A man loved his girlfriend very much and decided to tattoo her name, Wendy, onto his dick.

When his dick was erect the letters W E N D Y, were visible. However, when it was flaccid only the W and the Y could be seen.

One day the man goes on vacation to Jamaica and while on a tour of the beach he visits the Men's bathroom. As he is taking a piss, a big Jamaican man goes to use the urinal next to his. As the Jamaican whips it out, the man couldn't help but notice that the man's dick also happened to have a tattooed W and Y on it.

Curious, the man asks the Jamaican "Excuse me, I noticed your tattoo and I was wondering if your wife or girlfriend was also named Wendy like mine?

The Jamaican answered, "No mon! Why you ask?"

The man then said, "Oh it's just that mine also says W Y when it's not erect, and then when it's erect, it shows my girl's name W E N D Y."

The Jamaican smiled and said, "I see mon! I work for the tour company. When my dick grows it spells "WELCOME TO JAMAICA, THANK YOU FOR YOUR VISIT AND HAVE A NICE DAY"

The Castaways

A Canadian, an American and a Chinese man are stranded on a deserted island.

The Canadian tells the others that he will go forage for food. The American offers to seek out a source of fresh water. They then tell the Chinese man that he should scour the island for supplies. They split up to do their jobs and decide to meet up later.

When the Canadian and the American return, there is no sign of the Chinese man. The American had returned with 3 coconuts and the Canadian had found 4 mangos. Hours pass by, but still no word from their Chinese friend.

Later that evening as they start walking down a path in search for their friend, the Chinese man jumps out from behind the bushes and shouts,

"SUPPLIES!"

Tequila Shots

A young man walks up to the bar.

The bartender asks, "What will it be?"

The young man says, "Three tequila shots please!"

"Three shots! Celebrating something?" The bartender asks

The young man says, "Yep, my first blowjob!"

The bartender says, "Well that's certainly worth celebrating! Have a fourth tequila shot on me!"

The young man replies, "Thank you sir, but if the first three shots don't get rid of the taste, I seriously doubt a fourth will!"

The Pickle Slicer

John had worked at a pickle factory for many years.

One day he came home and confessed to his wife that he has been having terrible compulsions. He explained that as of very recently he has been having these irresistible desires to put his penis inside one of the pickle slicers at work.

Worried at this, his wife suggested he go see a therapist to help him overcome this crazy idea of his.

Several days later, John came home early looking completely devastated and with a pained expression on his face. His wife sensed something was wrong and asked what happened.

"You remember I told you a few days back I had this irresistible desire to put my penis inside one of the pickle slicers at work?"

"Yes, John, I do. Oh Lord! What have you done?"

"Yes, dear, I could not stop myself!"

"Oh my God John! What's happened to you?"

"I got fired."

"No, no, I mean what happened with the pickle slicer?"

"Oh well, she also got fired!"

Turner Brown

A little old man gets into an elevator and as the door closes behind him, he sees a very tall large black man standing next to the button panel.

The big, tall black man looks down at the little old man and says, "If you need to know, I'm 285 lbs., I am 7 foot 3 inches tall and yes I'm hung like a horse! Turner Brown!"

Upon hearing this, the little old man passes out and collapses to the floor of the elevator.

The big black man picks up the old man and helps him come to his senses.

The big black man asks the little old man, "What just happened to you?"

The little old man says, "I apologize, but what did you just say to me as I walked in?"

The big man again looks down and says "I just introduced myself! I said I'm 285 lbs., I am 7 foot 3 inches tall, I am hung like a horse and my name is Turner Brown!"

The little old man says, "Oh thank goodness! I thought I heard you say 'turn around!'"

The Miniskirt

"Mom! I'm going out with my girlfriends tonight!"

The mother replies, "Not with that miniskirt on! Go back to your room and put on something else or you're not leaving this house!"

"But mom, why?"

"Because it too damn short! That's why!"

"So what if it's too short!"

"Because then everyone can see your balls Timmy!" replied his mom.

Aroused

A wife is half asleep in bed when she hears her husband return home from work. After his shower, he climbs into bed and soon after she feels a slight caress on one of her legs. The husband then puts one of his hands down her waist and her back and moves it gently up and down.

The wife starts becoming aroused at this and then feels him slowly start to raise one of her legs. He proceeds to put one hand under her ankle and slowly moves it up her leg and up the back of her thigh and starts feeling around her buttocks.

The two hadn't had sex in a very long time, so now she starts feeling very excited and starts breathing heavily and writhing in the bed as he proceeds to explore further with his hands.

She flexes her legs and raises her hips in anticipation of her husband mounting her when suddenly he stops, turns, and settles down back on his side of the bed.

The wife, still aroused, but now a little confused asks, "What happened?"

"All set!" he replied.

"What do you mean…'all set'?" she asked.

"I found the TV remote!"

The Space Bar

My girlfriend just texted me:

'thespacebaronmyphoneisnotworkingcanyoup leasegivemeanalternative?'

I think I figured out what she wants, but does anyone know what "ternative" means?

I Can Build You a Boat

One guy is bragging to his friend, "I'm so good with my hands that if you just bring me 100 planks of wood and 1,000 nails, I can build you a boat!"

The friend says, "That's terrific! If you bring me your sister I can make the crew!"

The Black Suit

Two grieving widows arrive at the Funeral home to make final arrangements for their deceased husbands.

The first widow says to the mortician, "My husband was brought here wearing a blue suit, but his favorite is this black suit here. I'd really appreciate it if you could dress him in this black suit for the service tonight.

The mortician agrees and thanks the lady for bringing the man's favorite black suit.

The second widow walks in the office after the first one leaves and says, "Our son had brought a black suit earlier today for my husband, but he had always loved this blue suit. Is there any way you can have him dressed in this blue suit for his service tonight?"

The mortician assures her that this would not a problem and the second woman thanks him and leaves.

Later that evening the mortician is at the first man's service when the deceased's widow walks up and says, "Thank you so much for doing this. My husband looks wonderful in his black suit."

The mortician replies, "Of course, I was happy to do it. Oh and we did not need the suit you brought after all. I have it hanging out front and you can take it with you after the service."

"I don't understand. He is wearing his black suit now. Come let me show you."

"Oh no, no… I realize he is being shown with a black suit now, but let me explain. You see, right after you came in another woman showed up who had her husband in a black suit and she wanted him wearing a blue suit. So in the end all I had to do was swap the heads."

Fluctuations

A Chinese lady was trying to exchange her Yuan for US dollars at the bank.

She had been there the day before without incident, but today she was becoming very irritated with the teller.

She asked, "Why it change? Yesterday, I get two hunnat dolla fo Yuan. Today you only give me hunnat eighty? Why it change?"

The teller shrugged her shoulders and said, "Fluctuations."

The Chinese lady said, "Oh yea?! Well, Fluc you white people too!"

The Wine Critic

At the local vineyard, the master taster had just passed away and so the owner was forced to look for a replacement.

A very arrogant wine critic who had often given the vineyard mediocre and sometimes even poor wine reviews shows up to apply for the position.

The owner of the winery having no intention of hiring the man, decides to put the critic's skills to the test in an attempt to perhaps later discredit him should the critic publish yet another negative review.

He gives the critic a glass of wine to sample. The critic samples it and says, "It's a Muscat, three years old, grown on a north slope of the local area, and matured in steel containers. Low grade, but acceptable."

"Well, it is our Muscat," said the owner.

Another glass... "This is a Cabernet, eight years old, a south-western slope, oak barrels, matured at 8 degrees. Requires three more years for finest results."

"It is our finest Cabernet," says the owner.

A third glass... "It's a Pinot Blanc Champagne, high grade and very exclusive," the critic said calmly.

"It's a Pinot Blanc from a Vineyard in France," admitted the owner.

The owner was by now astonished! He went over to his young assistant, and quietly whispered something in her ear. She left the room, and returned a few minutes later with a glass full of urine.

The critic sampled it. "It's a blonde, 22 years old, three months pregnant and if I don't get this job I shall name the father!"

The Lifeguard

The lifeguard caught me taking a wiz by the deep end of the pool today. She yelled at me so loudly that I nearly fell in.

Visiting Israel

A Jewish banker in New York decides to send his son on a trip to Israel to absorb the culture of the homeland.

When the son returns, the father asks him to tell him all about the trip.

The son said, "Dad, I had a wonderful time in Israel. Oh, and you should know that while I was there I converted to Christianity."

"Oy vey," said the father. What the hell have I done? He thought to himself.

He decides to go ask his old friend Blake what to do. Blake said, "Funny you should ask. I too sent my son to Israel some years back, and he also came back a Christian. Perhaps we should go see the rabbi and ask him what we should have done differently."

So they went to see the rabbi. The rabbi said, "Funny you should ask. I too sent my son to Israel. He also came back a Christian. What is happening to our young people?

Later that afternoon at the temple the three of them pray and explain what had happened to their sons. They ask God for guidance.

Suddenly a Godly voice could be heard reverberating through the temple. The voice said, "Funny you should ask. I, too, sent my Son to Israel..."

Pants in the Family

A husband and wife arrive at the hotel on their wedding night.

Immediately both start undressing, and as the husband, who was a big, muscular man, removes his trousers, he tosses them to his young bride and commands her, "Here, put these on!"

Not knowing what he's up to, she tries them on, but they are way too big on her.

"I can't wear your pants. They're huge!" she says.

"That's right!" said the husband, "and don't you ever forget that! I'm the man who wears the pants in this family."

With that, she removes her panties and flips them onto his head. She says, "Fine! Now you try these on!"

He says "Hell no! I can't get into your panties!"

She replied, "That's right, and it's going to be that way until your attitude changes."

Jesus at the Restaurant

Jesus walks into a restaurant and says to the Maitre'd "Table for 26 please"

Confused, the Maitre'd does a quick head count, and says "Are we expecting more sir? I see there are only 13 of you."

Jesus replies "No we're not, but we're all going to sit on the same side."

The End

Follow M_H_Ballsych on twitter

http://www.twitter.com/M_H_Ballsych

Enjoyed this Book? Check out Volume 3 here:

http://www.amazon.com/gp/product/ B01DFTLZIS

(Bonus Material starts on next page)

Tweets from M. Harry Ballsych
(On Twitter)

Pussyfooting should be a PornHub genre and not just a cute cat reference!

Farts are like teaser trailers for the man event

A towel rack is like a pull-up bar for little people

Tequila Mockingbird would be a cool name for a drink! RIP #HarperLee

Is Papal excrement bona fide Holy Shit?

Things not to say to someone losing weight "Even your hair is thinner!"

Getting drunk and having sex you regret the next morning should be called a 'Bangover'.

What would be the response if science unveiled a vaccine for autism?

The Cocktopus would be a great name for a transvestite bar

If #Trump was POTUS he could choose the next justice of #SCOTUS via an Apprentice style reality TV show

As individuals, humans are simply amazing. As a race, we tend to be pretty terrible.

Perhaps the reason baby seals are so cute is that for many generations seal clubbers clubbed the ugly ones?

I wonder if auto-erotic asphyxiation works on other things. Like, this sandwich is pretty good, but what if I eat it while hanging myself?

You ever wonder if the guy next to you at the urinal is peeing louder so as to assert his dominance?

Flossing is like the opposite of masturbation. Nobody does it, but everyone says they do.

I wonder if nursing homes of the future will have X-Boxes and PlayStation consoles stashed next to the puzzles and checkerboards.

It's a damn good thing my heart is not as lazy as I am!

If Hillary becomes POTUS, does that make Monica the First Lady?

If a porn star says they had "a long hard day at work" they may not necessarily be complaining!

I used to be a male in a woman's body.

My ex always insisted I eat before grocery shopping. Now I jerk off before going on Tinder.

Choking on a lifesaver would seem like a very ironic way to die.

Seems like kids who cheat in school put more effort into it than kids who don't try at all!

I'm pretty confident that not a single one of my ancestors died as virgins.

If my dog licks its own ass, I seriously doubt it gives a flying fuck what flavor of dog food I buy.

Humans require years of training just to not shit themselves!

Seems to me like there is no way to "high five" little people without appearing condescending.

Why does "Shits and Giggles" sound OK, but "Sharts and Gargles" does not?

Homeopathy is actually highly effective at treating symptoms of dehydration.

I wonder if Andy's mom also has toys named 'Woody' and 'Buzz'?

Printed in Great Britain
by Amazon